WALK ME TO THE DOOR, LOVE

Notes written to the Beloved

in the first two years of grief

by BONNIE L. BAIRD

WALK ME TO THE DOOR, LOVE

Copyright © 2016 Bonnie Baird

Published by Bonnie Baird

Cover Art Design © Croco Designs

All rights reserved.

ISBN 978-0-9940973-5-4 (print book)

ISBN 978-0-9940973-2-3 (electronic book)

SELECT TITLES ALSO BY BONNIE L. BAIRD

Poetry

I SMELL STARS

LIGHTENING STRIKES

CLOSE TO THE UNDERTOW

Prose

SURVIVAL OF THE DANGLY GREEN PARROT EARRINGS

CD

WALK ME TO THE DOOR, LOVE

I SMELL STARS

Dedicated to Dave who taught my heart to sing.

ACKNOWLEDGEMENTS

Without the insightful listening of family and friends, and their encouragement to share my experience of grief with others, this book would not have emerged. Thank you to Laurie Omstead (listener for many years), Heather Veinotte (writing mentor and gifted author), Kathryn Lucking (recent friend and teacher), Barry Zacharias (my brother), Marion Olson (sister by marriage, Yeah!) and Matthew Baird (my son). Your presence and support brighten my days.

A special thank you to Frauke Spanuth of Croco Designs for the design of cover and contents. You are a master of discernment.

These poems are offered in the hope that they will help others who are grieving to understand that they are not alone. And that the journey is laced with beauty.

CONTENTS

WALK ME TO THE DOOR, LOVE

Walk me to the door, Love?
past all the rooms
and falling shades
along this corridor of us

YEAR ONE: IN YOUR WAKE

No Not Knowing

There are no moments of not knowing
even hovering ones

Waking to another shapeless day
slipping into sleep
in the meanderings of nightly phantasies
routines, responsibilities, plans
there is always the pressing awareness of you

not
a foot touch away in a duveted bed
familiar stranger dreaming your dreams
not
a voice closing the miles between
beginning and ending each day, stirring my heart
not
texting messages at ungodly hours
from your hospital room into the dark
You there?
You awake?

In this jarring place where you are
not
I'm fully awake now

(April)

GOOD WORK

You look asleep
the male version of Sleeping Beauty waiting for someone's kiss
on display for us
who need to see you once more
need a memory to replace the awful hospitalled ending
need to realize what has happened

your hands, so beat up in recent weeks,
beautifully tended to
strong hands that held so much so close for so long
the hollowing out of body
no longer evident
the familiar form given back
long enough to say goodbye

It is gift pure and simple
"You do good work," I tell the funeral director

(April)

TRUE TO FORM

I upgraded my room to one with a balcony
a few days before departure
despite the cost and my desire to be frugal
What the hell...they stuck me in a portholed room overlooking a
lifeboat
(rather apt, though)
and that's what you get for being a single in a doubles' world
Double the price for half the experience

I wrote about it in my journal to you who are no longer
"Just being true to form," I wrote,
"like that ketchup commercial we'd smile about, remember?
The one with the woman
looking across the table deep into her beloved's eyes, saying
'I've never settled for less than the best.' "

(April)

LAST NOTES OF OUR SONG

The last notes are dropping
one
by
one
into the rising conversations
and I, alone
among many,
keep on humming
that familiar last stanza

(May)

Iceberg

Moments into the channel
blue ice drifts by
not the blue of sky or sea but of time
trapped under tremendous weight

the lightness of snowflakes settled into layers into liquid into ice
into rivers of ice
into shards drifting towards open sea

We shudder to a stop
no tears in our steel to be seen
though one does think of the Titanic

one tenth is all we see
and what we see is blue
and what would it be like to plunge into the depths
unfathomable
see the hole where the ice penetrated
(for it did: everything is shifting beneath out feet)

see the whole frozen landscape

(May)

THE NATURE OF HOPE

It keeps shifting
like something winged and fragile and carried on the wind

like a moth hovering close to the porch light

This morning I found one wing torn off
pale and tinged with camouflage which in the end didn't help much
discarded fragment of a meal of something larger and carnivorous

Tomorrow there will be others clinging to the doorframe
waiting to lift on the morning breeze
some so blended in you can't see them until they move

And I wonder at their beauty, number, differences. Persistence.

(July)

TRACES

This is how I spend my days now:
searching

between the constellations
out on the waters early evening or first light
along overhung country roads

There a lone loon close to the rocky shore. Where is its mate?
A firefly hovering outside my window in the curtained dark.
Come close for a moment. Show me some light.
Old cigar wrappers surfacing on my path. Conversations past
swirl starward on a darkened deck, the end of a lit cigar, and your
smell all around me. Wrap me in you once more?

searching
for tangible and intangible connections
to keep me moving forward
closer to you

(July)

SOMETHING GOT EATEN

Something got eaten in the night
Something pale and green and winged
Something too large to hold in a hand
      but not apparently for something else on the prey for just
      such a meal, a creature
      bound to not flying except on strands of its own making
      or in dreams of being
      something else
The remains
can't be put together again
some are missing
the rest torn but lovely still

and where is the breath that would animate once more?
Gone
without so much as a sound
though there are ranges above and below which one can hear,
right?
just one quick movement
brutal and final
in the whispery night

(July)

The Corridor

"It won't last,"
echoes down the corridor
behind us
phrased, depending on circumstance, as sneer,
question, observation, prayer
persistent as shadow.

Yet

behind this door:
the roots we didn't put down except in one another
and in one child. No growing up and growing old with childhood
neighbours and friends. Not for us.

(Though the bad winds can take down even a firmly planted
solitary. I know that now.)

behind this one:
the paths taken.
Tangles of job loss and career shifts and treacherous places
where experience didn't help but cussedness did, and a sense of
humour.
The outer layers shed as the days heated up and the nights too.
Old bruises uncovered, new ones absorbed.
Waiting for the other to catch up or slow down.
Waiting for the healing salve of body, soul, and mind

touching
under the night skies.

behind this door:
the slogging years.
One step in front of the other.
One taking the lead, then the other.
Shifting the load gingerly across the chasms and
not looking down
and always the holding out of the hand to the other.
How did it last?

The last door:
the one I didn't want to approach
the one you walked through
head up, heart open
as family and friends watched in awe
as I did, wanting to come too.

How did we last beyond that first opening into us,
the blistering heat and the thrill of the new?

In the tall grasses, firelight, unending conversations
(we still talk, don't we?)
something was forged
strong as steel
unrelenting as light
something
unexpected.

(July)

HOME

It's strange to call a place no one is certain even exists
by such a name
yet many do
and I'm one now.

Home: remember the definition I gave someone with deep roots
in one place?
Home, I said, was anywhere you were My Love.

Home:
So when do I get to go home?

(August)

COUNSEL

I try to keep my own counsel now

After many failed attempts
I have discovered
that to speak about what I really see and feel and think
about so much swirling in your wake
is like walking nude in church

Some pretend I am wearing the Emperor's new clothes
some are shocked at the rawness
others have a theory about why such behaviour at such a time
most an opinion of what should be done which isn't

only the nude walkers are silent

It's tempting though
to sometimes burden another (is anyone out there listening?)
with questions and comments that sound like questing for
solution
There is no solution to this. God is not impotent, only silent. And
the desire for justice, a bit of cosmic compassion, is an ancient
one.

In the speaking of such matters, there is always
a lingering sense of betrayal of something
too much of us

Oh, Love, come sit beside me in the starry night
as we figure out our little patch of the universe, spout what-ifs
and marvel at the complexity of it all
filters off (no topic too sacred), imaginations spiralling

who else could I ever go to and not be found wanting?

(August)

THE LAST FIRST

Here at the inn
old trees overlook the Mersey
Adirondack chairs draw up close to the water's edge

And do you remember
that hot day in Acadia*
walking past all those beautifully groomed couples
who had doubtless reserved their chairs
for the better view weeks before

The bow-tied server who took us—
sweaty and mud splattered and dishevelled
after the long arduous hike
a few flies buzzing about us
nothing to recommend us and certainly no reservations—

to two chairs set off by themselves
at the water's edge

tea in translucent porcelain pots, out-of-the-oven
popovers and homemade strawberry preserves
staining our lips, running over the edges
onto white linen napkins

no one to obscure the wonder before us

Will it be like this, do you suppose,
when we meet again?

(September)

*national park

YEAR TWO: CRY HOLY

After Our Friend's Death

The sum of all this dying
lies buried under the snow
and a layer of ice more than a foot thick

birds of prey are praying for a little sustenance
a few eagles gather water's edge feasting on a deer carcass

but pickings generally are slim and prayers are dropping from
trees
malnourished, talons refusing to let go the higher view

Snow continues to accumulate

(April)

My Name

My name is the shape of twisted
driftwood
remnants of shipwrecks with no survivors
made into a doll's cradle
rocking in the stormy night

(May)

FADE

I find my rings scattered across the pale green sheets
first light
as the last traces linger of the bridge collapsing and our mud-
embedded car is winched up
immersion pouring off

no memory of removing these circular bands
only of standing on the bank plotting how to continue

Three rings for the time we've known

dematerializing
in the fade

(May)

FACE

I look up
into a face etched weary from caring for another who couldn't
be saved
either

Almost a year and a half in

and though the body responds primordially
(Does the body ever fully forget?)
eyes averted: hard to look into such beauty and pain
tongue thickening with unsaying
skin vibrantly aware of proximity

it is too soon

the common ground is abyss
difficult to navigate
impossible to span

(May)

Spiraling at the Cottage

Heavy the heart here
Love
heavy your passing

heavy the starry light

Predator and prey and one bright collision of blood in the snow
Cosms micro and macro spinning in an endless circle and we
with them

For all that is here now
for all that once was
shall we cry "Holy"
and be done?

(June)

STILL THE NIGHT

It is still here tonight
no voices, rustlings, swooshes

no fireflies either (though this is the season)
except one
there
on the edge of the pines
flashing signals no mate's receiving

everything still as though
paused
to consider
what happens next

(June)

ACHE

The familiar ache is here
turning ever so slightly in the chest
Good to feel again
even this
Good to remember
us

(July)

BEARINGS

On this trek we began with so much energy, expectation
I've taken a side route and you
are nowhere in sight

Even without a map or GPS
your sense of direction was always better than mine
(something in the blood honed to home)

Just got to keep moving
keep looking for signs
(I haven't seen any in awhile)

Hope you will be there

(August)

Sale of the Cottage

Our son sees only a door closing
the key turned for the last time
no going back

Memories are persistent, though, as little boys
getting up for a glass of water
sneaking back into the centre of all the action
calling out for one last story
one last tuck in
one last hug or rough and tumble till the bed shakes and you
collapse in a heap
ready to let go the day with all its bruises and glory

No lock on that

(August)

THREE WOMEN IN A BAR

Three women seated in a bar
one turns to the others, says:
"And here we are."

and she isn't speaking about
Air Canada grounding us once again
connections made between strangers
during crisis

the common ground
lies deeper

two widows of different generations
one widow by Alzheimer's
("I told them not to call me if anything happens.")

over red wine
exploring commonalities
in a world of aloneness

(November)

COMMON LANGUAGE

Somewhere in the far east our niece
is studying Arabic

painstakingly unlearning what she has picked up in dialects

when she is finally fluent in this ancient scholarly tongue
she may have forgotten how to speak the common language

Will it be so for me
wrestling with the hieroglyphs
of grief?

(November)

THRESHOLD

Standing on the threshold
I feel like turning around

Outside, though it's cold,
at least I know the terrain

I did so once before, remember?
on a cold October night
too many years ago to count
stood there as the music swelled and everyone turned to face me

that moment felt like a closing in
doors shutting I would never open again
yet there you stood
up ahead
inviting me in

If I step forward
this time
can I leave the door open, just a bit?

(January)

About the Author

Bonnie Baird is a writer, priest, and blessed mom and grandma currently living along Nova Scotia's South Shore.